New York Journal

Liz Corcoran & Leta Keens

MQP

CONTENTS

WELCOME TO THE BIG APPLE

HISTORIC NEW YORK

New York is an ugly city, a dirty city. Its climate is a scandal, its politics are used to frighten children, its traffic is madness, its competition is murderous. But there is one thing about it – once you have lived in New York and it has become your home, no place else is good enough!

John Steinbeck (1902–68)

EARLY NEW YORK

Henry Hudson

*T*oday's New York sets a fast and furious pace, a dramatic difference to life 400 years ago. The navigator Giovanni da Verrazano was the first European visitor. He sailed the *Dauphane* into New York harbour in 1524 searching for the fabled Northwest Passage. It was not until 1609 that the Englishman Henry Hudson, employed by the Dutch East India Co, journeyed to the area and charted the course of the river that was later to take his name.

In the following decade a trickle of Europeans arrived here. In 1614 the area between the Delaware and Connecticut Rivers became known as New Netherland. In 1624, the Dutch West India Co mustered settlers who arrived first on Nutten Island (now Governor's Island) and then Manhattan Island.

The settlement was called New Amsterdam and by 1626 there were more than 200 settlers involved in farming and trade, and fledgling settlements were being established. The land was rich in crops, game was plentiful and the settlement flourished.

PLANNING NOTES

The Indians

Relations with the Indians were by no means peaceful in the
17th century as the colonists attempted to control the
indigenous peoples. After a number of bloody skirmishes,
Peter Stuyvesant, a peg-legged veteran of Dutch colonies in
Brazil and Curaçao, arrived in New Amsterdam in 1647 to
restore peace and coax along trade. Among other things
Stuyvesant introduced the first municipal government and
ordered fortifications to be built at today's **Wall Street**, but
his authoritarian stance against religious freedom and the
taxes expected by the Dutch colonial masters irked many of
the colonists. When four English warships sailed into New
Amsterdam harbour in 1664 to claim the
island for King Charles II, the colony, its
defences inadequate, put up no
resistance. New Amsterdam
became New York.

To say something of the Indians, there is now but few upon the Island, and those few no ways hurtful but rather serviceable to the English, and it is to be admired, how strangely they have decreased by the Hand of God, since the English first settling of those parts; for since my time, where there were six towns, they are reduced to two small Villages, and it hath been generally observed, that where the English come to settle, a Divine Hand makes way for them, by removing or cutting off the Indians either by Wars one with the other, or by some raging mortal Disease.

Daniel Denton, *A Brief Description of New York: Formerly Called New Netherland*, 1670

George Washington

REVOLUTION & INDEPENDENCE 1776

*I*n the 18th century New York was an important harbour city and increasingly cosmopolitan, with European settlers and a large slave population. In 1725 the *New York Gazette* became the city's first newspaper, rivalled in 1733 by John Peter Zenger's *New York Weekly Journal* which openly criticised the colonial government. Zenger was imprisoned for libel but later acquitted. His case provided the basis for the First Amendment to the Constitution which allows for freedom of the press.

The seeds of the American War of Independence were sown in the mid-18th century as citizens became disgruntled by high taxes. A group of revolutionaries, known as the Sons of Liberty, led their first uprising against British troops stationed in the city in 1765. Throughout the next decade friction remained between the troops and their supporters and the Sons of Liberty.

First Impressions

Washington triumphant

After the Declaration of Independence in July 1776, New Yorkers tore down a statue of George III on **Bowling Green** in Lower Manhattan and British troops under General William Howe arrived in force in New York harbour. The revolutionaries did not fare well in battle and later that year George Washington and his troops were defeated at Fort Washington and forced to retreat from the island which became a haven for loyalists. The British finally quit the city in 1783, defeated in the war, and on 4 December Washington rode triumphant. 'I am not only retiring from all public engagements, but am retiring within myself,' he told his troops. Famous last words! Just over five years later Washington took the oath as the first President of the United States at the original Federal Hall, on **Wall Street**.

Conference House

American patriots Benjamin Franklin, John Adams and Edmund Rutledge met here with British Admiral Richard Howe in September 1776 to discuss a peaceful resolution to the War of Independence. Negotiations failed and the war continued until 1783.

Fraunces Tavern

The present building, dating from 1907, is a reconstruction of the original tavern. Its reconstruction marks America's first attempts to preserve the country's heritage. The original tavern, the Queen Charlotte, named after George III's bride was built in 1719. It was later re-named after proprietor Samuel Fraunces in recognition of his service to American prisoners of war following the outbreak of the American Revolution. The original tavern had a chequered history; in 1775 a cannonball was fired through its roof from the British ship *Asia*. Later George Washington bade farewell to his troops there in 1783.

The replica building houses a museum with a constantly changing exhibition of prints and paintings from early American history.

IMMIGRATION

Multitudes flocked into this city and into other
cities on our Atlantic border to encounter only
want and wretchedness to an extent that baffled
our means of alleviation: friendless, moneyless,
unable to procure employment, crushed in spirit
and emaciated in body, many sought refuge in the
alms houses.

Irish Emigration Society to Ireland, 1843

*B*y 1820 New York was America's largest city with
Manhattan's population almost 125,000. In the
decades that followed, immigrants from Europe fleeing
persecution, poverty or famine swelled the population, and in
their wake established New Yorkers shifted uptown. When the
Erie Canal connecting the Great Lakes with the Hudson
River opened in 1825 facilitating the transport of goods, New
York's position as the pre-eminent American city was
established. By 1860 the population in Manhattan was over
800,000.

NOTES

The 'melting pot'

Since the 17th century when the first German, Dutch and English immigrants came to New York, the city has been home to a wide mix of ethnic groups. By 1746 20% of the population were African slaves. The Irish settlers arrived soon after the Germans, driven by the severe potato famines at home. Later, millions of German and East European Jews persecuted in the pogroms arrived. The Chinese have come in large numbers since the 19th century, as have the

Puerto Ricans and the Hispanics in this century. African-Americans accounted for six per cent of the population earlier this century. Today, with the addition of Caribbeans, that figure is higher . The Italians have formed a large community in New York since the 1930s.

Ellis Island

Ellis Island was the first port of call for 12 million immigrants to the States from 1892 to 1954, though it was only used sporadically in later years. Over a million people entered the United States through Ellis Island in 1907, the peak year of immigration. Herded like cattle into pens in the building; bewildered, and often speaking no English, they were checked for diseases, indications of mental illness – anything that might prevent them from earning a living. The majority passed and made their way to the doors marked 'Push for New York'.

19TH-CENTURY MANSIONS & TENEMENTS

In Boston they ask, How much does he know? in
Philadelphia, Who were his parents? in New York,
How much is he worth?

Mark Twain (1835–1910)

*G*reat fortunes were amassed by New York's elite in the
mid to late 19th century and many refer to this period
as the 'Gilded Age'. The Vanderbilts owned railroads, the
Astors had vast tracks of real estate, Andrew Carnegie
controlled steel and J Pierpont Morgan dominated the world
of finance. Their houses, many of which lined **Fifth Avenue**,
were like palaces, full of exquisite works of art, even whole
period rooms, plucked from grand European homes. No
expense was spared in furnishings or in the sumptuous parties
held and attended by the favoured '400', a list of eminent
New Yorkers, drawn up by Caroline Astor, *The* Mrs Astor.
Others, with a philanthropic bent, delighted in giving their
money away.

NOTES

Frick Collection

This Beaux Arts mansion built for Henry Clay Frick in 1914 reflects the lavish lifestyle lived by rich New Yorkers. Frick made his fortune as an industrialist, becoming a millionaire by the impressive age of 30. His mansion at 1 East 70th Street at **Fifth Avenue** was bequeathed to the nation on his death. The mansion is unique in its reflection of early 20th century bourgeois taste. The museum contains Frick's priceless collection of furniture, Limoges enamels, and old master paintings, including works by Turner, Constable, Vermeer, Hals, Rembrandt, Titian, Bellini and Holbein.

Andrew Carnegie

> A man who dies rich dies thus disgraced.
>
> Andrew Carnegie (1835–1919)

Andrew Carnegie migrated from Scotland when he was 13 and worked his way up the economic and social ladder to become one of America's kings of industry. He monopolised the steel industry and when he returned to Scotland on his retirement he set about giving away most of his vast fortune. By the end of his life he had rid himself of some $350 million, endowing **Carnegie Hall** to the country. Home to the **New York Philharmonic** for many years, the building soon became a symbol of international success in both classical and modern repertoires. In addition Carnegie's generosity provided over $5 million for 65 library buildings in the city.

Tenements

It was a wretched life for recently arrived immigrants. They were delivered, says Henry Roth in his book *Call it Sleep* (1934), 'from the stench and throb of the steerage to the stench and throb of New York tenements' and in between were processed like cattle on **Ellis Island**. Early tenement buildings, known as 'railroad apartments' because they were simply a string of rooms with no corridors, were dingy affairs with windowless inner rooms. Families shared communal privies and few buildings had running water. In 1867 there were attempts to improve the filthy conditions and laws demanded a privy for every 20 tenants as minimum and better standards of ventilation.

By 1901 two thirds of the population, around 2.3 million people, lived in these buildings. In 1890 Jacob A Riis published his book *How the Other Half Lives*, which did much to raise public consciousness about the plight of the poor in the Lower East Side.

Lower East Side Tenement Museum

Built in 1863 and now preserved as a museum, the Lower East Side Tenement Museum at 97 Orchard Street reconstructs the squalid conditions endured by many New Yorkers at the turn of the 19th century. Running water, flush toilets and electricity were only installed in 1905. This eye-opening museum is a good point from which to explore the colourful neighbourhood.

Paved with gold

Alistair Cooke, eminent British author and social historian asked one immigrant if he was disappointed that New York's streets were not paved with gold: 'But there was gold,' he said, 'to us. There were markets groaning with food and clothes. There were streetcars all over town. You could watch the automobiles. There was no military on horseback and no whips. The neighbors were out in the open, trading and shouting, enjoying free fights. And to a boy like me it was a ball, a friendship club. The streets were an open road.'

Alistair Cooke, *America*, 1973

It began singing in my heart, the music of the whole Hester Street. The pushcart peddlers yelling their goods, the noisy playing of the children in the gutter, the women pushing and shoving each other with their market baskets – all that was only hollering noise before melted over me like a new beautiful song.

Anzia Yezierska, *Bread Givers*, 1925

THE ROARING TWENTIES
& THE DEPRESSION

Duke Ellington

*N*ew York in the 1920s was a heady, spirited place which even Prohibition, introduced nationwide by the government in 1920 prohibiting the consumption of alcohol, could not dampen. New Yorkers' thirst for life could be slaked at one of 32,000 speakeasies. Wall Street boomed and women got the vote.

It was a time when **Harlem**, a village surrounded by farmland only half a century before, came into its own as black artists, writers, musicians and political activists arrived in droves attracted by the Harlem Renaissance, and white New Yorkers scampered up town to revel in 'the Negro vogue'. Prominent black New Yorkers at the time included W E B Du Bois, a writer and the director of the National Association for the Advancement of Colored People, and writer James Weldon Johnson.

At the famous **Cotton Club** Duke Ellington entertained white audiences, and the dancehalls jived with the Charleston, the Black Bottom, the Lindy Hop and the Shuffle.

NOTES

NOTES

The Harlem Renaissance

The Harlem Renaissance was a black literary and artistic movement of the 1920s. It did much to raise black American consciousness in the years before the Depression. An important, although earlier work by W E B Du Bois was *The Souls of Black Folk* (1903). Other writers to come into prominence include James Weldon Johnson (*The Autobiography of an Ex-Colored Man*, 1912), Carl Van Vechten (*Nigger Heaven*, 1926) and poet Langston Hughes (*The Weary Blues*, 1926).

Prominent painters included Aaron Douglas who was noted for his book illustrations and cover of the black publication *Opportunity and Crisis*.

Schomburg Center for Research in Black Culture

Arthur A Schomburg's remarkable collection relating to black American history has been housed in this former New York Public Library building since 1926. It was a meeting place for Harlem Renaissance writers such as W E B Du Bois, Langston Hughes and Zora Neale Hurston. Over the years the Center has hosted countless poetry readings, seminars and literary gatherings.

The Wall Street Crash

The stock market crash, on 29 October 1929, was a bludgeon to the exuberance of the 20s. Sixteen million shares were desperately traded on 'Black Tuesday', as the day was dubbed. Huge sums of money were lost, companies went out of business and New York, along with the rest of America, was plunged into depression. In **Central Park** squatter settlements housed those who had lost their homes and up to one quarter of New Yorkers were out of work.

Mayor Fiorello La Guardia persuaded the White House to fund many city projects including roads, schools, parks and highways under The New Deal. The Works Progress Administration (WPA) provided emergency employment to hundreds of thousands of New Yorkers, mostly in construction, and as a result New York pulled through the Depression.

20TH-CENTURY
NEW YORK

*A*fter World War II New York became host to the newly formed **United Nations**, which occupies a stretch along the East River donated by John D Rockefeller and is not officially part of the USA or its laws. The multinational body, which is dedicated to global peace and economic development, only had to look to its own backyard to find an area in dire need of help. During the 1960s and '70s serious riots broke out in **Harlem**, by now severely run down with high crime and unemployment rates.

Frank Lloyd Wright completed the remarkable **Guggenheim Museum** in 1959. In 1968 the **Lincoln Center** complex was opened. In 1990, the population had reached a staggering 7 million and more than 80 languages could be heard. New York is considered by many to be America's true capital, setting national trends in art, design, literature, fashion, music and drama, among others.

Ed Koch
former mayor

NOTES

Contemporary arts and letters

New York has always boasted a vital arts scene. The 1950s and '60s were important times for art in New York, and it remains today the contemporary art capital of the world. New York has been the city of the *avant garde* and the radical. All that was new in the arts could be found in the fabulous loft gallery spaces in SoHo and Tribeca. Composers like John Cage and Philip Glass were involved in impromptu multimedia 'happenings'. In theatre both off-Broadway and off off-Broadway provided mesmerising performances by new playwrights as well as non-traditional adaptations of the classics by groups such as the **Living Theatre**, the **Performance Group** and the **Wooster Group**. At the **Judson Dance Theater** in the '60s a new dance language was forged by choreographers including Steve Paxton, David Gordon and Lucinda Childs. The literary scene after the war moved to the lively west side while new poets like LeRoi Jones and Robert Creeley settled on the east side. It seemed that anybody who was anybody was in New York or at least there in spirit and today New York continues to sizzle with creativity and ideas.

United Nations

The United Nations (UN) Building was designed by a multi-national team that included Le Corbusier, Oscar Neimeyer and Sven Markelius. There are guided tours daily of the main chambers, including the General Assembly and the Security Council. The site includes a number of artworks, many donated by member states and among them a sculpture in the shape of a knotted gun by Karl Fredrik Ruertersward and a Peace Bell made from coins from many nations, donated by Japan. Most of these sculptures, mosaics, murals and artworks have peace and unity as their underlying theme.

The UN building is officially in an international zone and is not part of the US. As such it has its own postal system and postage stamps.

NOTES

Particularities of New York

FOOD

*I*n a city where anything goes and innovation is expected, it is hardly surprising that many new dishes and drinks were tasted here for the first time. Some were more successful than others. The first Bloody Mary was mixed at the **St Regis Hotel** and the Kamikaze at **Les Pyrenees**. Veal parmigiana and pasta primavera apparently made their debut in the Big Apple, as did bagels, blintzes, English muffins and the ice-cream sandwich. Hot dogs became popular thanks to **Nathan's** at Coney Island. Not to be missed is the New York cheesecake, both Jewish and Italian styles, and of course there's the corned beef sandwich, the tuna salad sandwich, in fact all New York overstuffed sandwiches. Try New York's famous delis like the **Carnegie**, the **Stage Deli**, or the **Second Avenue Delicatessen** and for the ultimate treat go to **Katz's Deli** where the pastrami is unforgettable. Buy your bagels at **Essa Bagel** or **H&H Bagel** and wander through the heady food aisles at **Zabar's**, **Balducci's** or **Dean & DeLuca**.

For a slow brew stop in at **P J Clarkes**, **McSorley's Old Alehouse**, or **The Ear Inn**. You could try a chic drink in a very Philippe Stark setting at the **Royalton Hotel**, or sip a traditional sherry in the **Algonquin Hotel** lobby.

For that special New York ambience do the **Oak Room and Bar** at the **Plaza**. The **Tenth Street Lounge** is a great spot for good drinks and there are plenty of interesting faces to look at. If it's a business drink or even a business lunch head for the **Monkey Bar** in midtown. Hot tips in New York mean either the stock market or a restaurant. New Yorkers spend hours not only enjoying restaurants but talking about them afterwards. Some very special New York eateries include **Gotham Bar & Grill**, **Union Square Café**, **Grand Central Oyster Bar**, **Sign of the Dove**, the **Mesa Grill**, **Café des Artistes**, **Gramercy Tavern**, **Patria** and **Tribeca Grill**. For special ocassions don't miss **Chanterelle** and the great food at **Le Cirque**. Delicious but expensive sushi can be savoured at **Nobu** in Tribeca and if you're in the mood for an authentic steak frite and good burgundy go to **Les Halles**. Grab a delicious quick bite or brunch at **E Js Luncheonette**, **America**, or the **Kiev Luncheonette** (borscht from heaven). **Planet Hollywood** is a hoot, as is the **Hard Rock Café** and whatever happens go to Chinatown for the famous **Golden Unicorn** Dim Sum.

NOTES

WEATHER

There is nothing wishy-washy about Manhattan seasons. In winter Arctic blasts whip up the avenues and snow piles high on the pavements, forcing New Yorkers to embark on a climbing expedition every time they cross the road, often negotiating the added obstacles of no longer-wanted Christmas trees and wreaths. The two benevolent seasons, spring and fall, rush in and out as if they have no place being in the city, but the New York summer has a special life of its own, heralded in by smells seeping up through cracks in the street and drips from air conditioners overhead, and heat and dust so relentless that the few New Yorkers who have not escaped to the sea feel caked for months with a layer of grit, and dream of snow flurries.

SOUNDS

The city's hum and buzz, the clinking of capstans,
the ringing of bells, the barking of dogs, the
clattering of wheels, tingled in the listening ear.
Charles Dickens, *American Notes*, 1842

*W*ailing sirens, satisfyingly familiar from movies and TV cop shows, do not slow down for the night and the seats at the **Angelika Film Center** on Houston Street vibrate with the low rumble of subway trains way below. On summer evenings rap music pounds out from open car windows, and steam hisses up through manholes. Steel drums jangle harshly down the long tunnel at the Port Authority Bus Terminal and at the end of a long, cold winter, New Yorkers stand mesmerised at the water's edge at **Battery Park City**, listening to the gentle fizz of ice floes on the Hudson.

It is the power of the most extravagant of cities, rejoicing, as with the voice of morning, in its might, its fortune, its unsurpassable conditions, and imparting to every object and element, to the motion and expression of every floating, hurrying, panting thing, to the throb of ferries, and tugs, and the splash of waves and the play of winds and the glint of lights and the shrill of whistles and the quality and authority of breeze-borne cries – all practically, a diffused, wasted clamour of detonations.

Henry James, *The American Scene*, 1907

BASEBALL

When things were going badly for them,
they did not complain but bore down harder.
They were civilised and had a naturally
assured way about them. That was the true
New York quality of spirit. Not bumhood.
  E L Doctorow, describing the Yankees baseball
    team, *World's Fair*, 1985

*T*here is some dispute as to the precise date and place
of the birth of baseball, but without a doubt Manhattan
and Brooklyn played a major role in its early life. In 1846
rules for the New York game, the forerunner of modern
baseball, were issued by members of the Knickerbocker Club,
an organisation of professional workers from the Madison
Square area. It did not take long for the game to sweep
through the eastern part of the States and during the 1850s
it was referred to as the national sport. Its popularity
gradually spread throughout the country, but its audiences

were boosted rapidly when games started being broadcast on TV in 1939. Today the two major New York teams are the Yankees and the Mets, both of which play home games (at **Yankee** and **Shea Stadiums**, respectively) during the baseball season from April to October. As well as the game originating in the city, two important baseball traditions started in New York in the early part of the 20th century – New York spectators were the first to eat hot dogs at the game around 1900 and the first to hear the song 'Take Me Out to the Ball Game' in 1908.

ROLLERBLADING
& RUNNING

*A*re New York's rollerbladers insane? Quite possibly. It is hard enough negotiating New York's streets on foot, or even in a car, but there are those who seriously think the best way to get from A to B is to speed through the traffic on skates – the wrong way and with cellular phones glued to their ears. The less certifiable head to **Central Park** to whiz around a circuit or sashay and shimmy at the roller disco at weekends or at the **Wollman Rink** in the summer. The real show-offs perform on a short strip parallel to Central Park West where, in front of an appreciative audience, they negotiate a makeshift slalom with amazing dexterity.

Running

No matter if it's rain or shine, winter or summer, day or night New Yorkers love to run. You can see them in their trend-setting designer tights or baggy grey sweats in the parks, on the streets or in high-tech health clubs. Often they will be attached to headphones. They run alone, in groups, with dogs and even pushing baby strollers. They are out there red-faced and sweating with expressions of beatific virtuousness because they know they are staying as young and fit as they can possibly be.

The New York City Marathon

One day every October the transport of choice in New York is legs, lots of them, and preferably fast ones. Since 1970, runners from all over the world have participated in the NY City Marathon. At first the race was run in **Central Park**, which did not offer much variety in terms of scenery, but now the 20,000-plus men and women who cover the distance can set foot in all five New York boroughs, starting at one end of the **Verrazano Narrows Bridge** in **Staten Island** and finishing near the **Tavern on the Green** on the west side of Central Park.

NOTES

COCKROACHES

*A*hh, the ubiquitous cockroach. He found New York City to his liking. Even the most pristine of the city's apartments is vulnerable to an invasion – they greet you in the morning by the sink and scurry across your tv at night.

But these creepy crawlies with their dark shiny armour-plating prove mighty little fighters. When hefty encyclopedias and boots will not do the trick there are plenty of insecticide sprays on the market. But perhaps the best method of ensuring a roach-free existence is to use poisonous bait, say the Roach Motel – a veritable cockroach Norman Bates. It entices the little beasties with irresistible whiffs and they enter a box where they meet their maker. As the packaging says, 'they check in, but they can't check out'.

A huge old refrigerator stood in the room. I wrenched open the door and there they were, the little darlings. It was an entire cockroach convention. I'd seen one roach earlier gazing down the plughole, but I knew his pals had to be concealed elsewhere, doubtless rehearsing a surprise party for me.

Stephen Brook, *New York Days, New York Nights*, 1984

CABS, BUSES
& SUBWAYS

The traffic seemed to come down Broadway out of
the sky, where the hot spokes of the sun rolled
from the south. Hot, stony odors rose from the
subway grating in the street.
Saul Bellow, *Seize the Day*, 1956

Cabs

The preferred occupation of new immigrants can prove
hazardous to the unaware. Drivers by law must have passed
exams demonstrating a knowledge of the city's geography, and
an understanding of English, but this cannot be guaranteed.
All New York's licensed cabs are yellow, hailing 'gypsy' cabs
can be dangerous.

Subways

New York's subway offers a cheap, convenient and relatively
fast way to travel across the city. A single-price token pays
for any distance. The system has been upgraded in recent

years, and travel during most times of the day or night is relatively safe.

Buses

New York's buses run a non-stop 24-hour service on many of the city's routes. Frequency though is reduced outside of peak hours. Although it's slow, travelling by bus has many advantages – it's cheap; but have the right change or a token handy when getting on a bus, it's convenient, clean, air-conditioned, a very safe way to travel and a good way to see the sights and the people close up.

PARADES

*P*arades have been a feature of New York City life for three hundred years. They were military in origin or commemorated events such as Independence.

The Chinese New Year kicks off the annual procession of street parades, when the celebrations among the Chinese New Yorkers include dragon parades, fireworks and food throughout **Chinatown**. For the fit and hardy, the annual run up the 1575 steps of the **Empire State Building** takes place in February. The first **St Patrick's Day Parade**, which today attracts over 150,000 marchers and sees **Fifth Avenue** awash with green, took place in 1766. **Earth Day** on the 20/21 March quickly follows, when the UN peace bell is rung as the sun crosses the equator. On Easter Sunday a parade runs up **Fifth Avenue** from 44th to 59th Streets. The annual parade is best seen from **St Patrick's Cathedral**. Hundreds of food stalls line the streets from 37–57th Streets for the **Ninth Avenue International Food Festival** in mid May. The **Mermaid Parade** at **Coney Island** held in June, swims with revellers dressed to indulge their fishy fantasies.

The city's most colourful celebration is the **Puerto Rico Day Parade**. Decorated floats and marching bands take to the streets on the first Sunday in June. **Harlem Week** in early August is the world's largest black and Hispanic festival of music, dance, exhibitions, and sport. The street festival which runs between 125th and 135th Streets includes a carnival of gospel, jazz, arts and food. Another favourite is the **Macy's** sponsored **Thanksgiving Day Parade** that takes place at the end of November between **Central Park West** and the famous department store on **Broadway**. This parade heralds the festive season with a succession of themed floats and huge balloons.

A quirkier celebration on the streets of Manhattan is the annual **Hallowe'en Parade** – a night of ghoulish frolics along **Sixth Avenue. The Christmas Tree Lighting Ceremony** at the **Rockefeller Center** at the start of December sets the Christmas season rolling. Five miles of lights are wrapped around the huge tree. See in the New Year in **Times Square** when a huge lighted ball is lowered over the crowds on the stroke of midnight.

NEW YORK SKYLINE

Skyscrapers

> A hundred times I have thought New York is a
> catastrophe, and fifty times: it is a beautiful
> catastrophe.
>> Le Corbusier, architect (1887–1965)

Manhattan's gentle natural topography was blasted and
bulldozed long ago to make way for an altogether more
dramatic man-made skyline of 'reach to the sky' edifices
separated by deep vertical-sided canyons. The skyline is
instantly recognisable, with the soaring twin towers of the
World Trade Center dominating the downtown area and the
Empire State Building holding court in midtown
surrounded by a cluster of worthy courtiers, including the
Chrysler Building and the **General Electric Building**.

In early Colonial times New York was a low-rise ramshackle
settlement that stretched to today's **Wall Street**, but by the
mid-19th century, as the city prospered, elegant buildings and
soaring spires could be glimpsed through a filigree of ships'
masts by those who sailed into the harbour.

At the end of the 19th century demand for office space in
the cramped downtown area of Manhattan increased and
architects looked to the skies. Manhattan was blessed with the
perfect geology and that, along with innovations in elevator
technology, made seven-storey buildings, then eleven and

then 20 possible. Skyscraper 'technology' itself, a steel skeleton clad, say, in brick, stone or terracotta, was used in the **Flatiron Building** in 1902, which occupies a unique triangular site. As buildings got progressively higher, concerns were voiced about the lack of light reaching the streets below. The architect Ernest Flagg suggested that buildings should be 'set back', the tower only covering 25 per cent of the total site area of the building, but zoning laws were not enacted until 1916.

> In the early months of 1903 I stood spell-bound … before the Flatiron Building … It appeared to be moving toward me like the bow of a monster ocean steamer, a picture of new America in the making.
>
> The Flatiron is to the United States what the Parthenon was to Greece.
>
> Alfred Stieglitz, 1903, in Dorothy Norman, *Alfred Stieglitz: An American Seer*, 1973

NOTES

Art Deco

> The city is full of gags and wisecracks, one-man
> shows and lineups, variety acts of every
> description, buildings that will go to any length,
> and generally do, for a share of the limelight, a
> laugh, a round of applause.
>
> Joe Friedman, *Inside New York*, 1993

In the '20s and '30s some of New York's most famous
skyscrapers were built: the **Chrysler Building**, the **Empire
State Building**, the **General Electric Building**, and **The
Chanin** are all superb examples of Art Deco design. After
World War II architects embraced the 'international style'
with a slew of modernist glass-sided buildings, many with
accompanying plazas.

If you think of the skyline as headline news, then the
colossal 110-storey twin towers of the **World Trade Center**,
among the most recent additions, are huge exclamation
marks. There is, of course, the small print too, which should
not be missed: the skyscape is awash with pseudo antiquities –
Grecian and Roman temples and Egyptian ziggurats (often
hiding water towers), while the lobbies of many buildings
house ornate elevator doors, fancifully painted or mosaic
ceilings and decorative mail chutes.

81

NOTES

The Chrysler Building

The Chrysler Building, completed in 1930 and for a brief time the tallest building in the world, is an Art Deco gem. Walter P Chrysler, head of the automobile company, suggested the steel eagle-head gargoyles and winged radiator-cap adornments as well as the illuminated chevron helmet that provides a cheery beacon for the city. The lobby is stunning, lined with marble, exquisite marquetry elevator doors and an ornate painted ceiling. It was originally used as the showroom for Chrysler cars.

The Woolworth Building

When Frank Winfield Woolworth decided to build headquarters for his five and dime empire he told architect Cass Gilbert, 'I do not want a mere building. I want something that will be an ornament to the city.' He got his wish. The Woolworth Building, on **Broadway** and Park Place, with its ornate terracotta façade and cruciform, mosaic lobby, is a neo-gothic masterpiece and was dubbed a 'cathedral of commerce' in 1913 when it was completed. Nine hundred guests were invited to the opening and, on cue, President Woodrow Wilson flicked a button in the White House that turned on all the lights. At 240m (792ft) the Woolworth remained the highest building in New York until overtaken by the Chrysler in 1929. *The New York Times* said the building 'stretches up, imperturbably august, a conquest of architecture. It storms the sky.'

Crammed on the narrow island the million-
windowed buildings will jut glittering, pyramid on
pyramid like the white cloudhead above the
thunderstorm.

John Dos Passos, *Manhattan Transfer*, 1925

Lever House and the Seagram Building

Two striking modernist structures are on **Park Avenue**.

Lever House, which was built in 1952 for the soap powder
manufacturers, is a shimmering steel and glass affair, two
rectangular blocks on top of each other, reflecting the
flamboyant stonework of the **Racquet Club** opposite.

The Seagram Building, designed by Ludwig Mies van der
Rohe and completed in 1958, has a bronze and glass exterior
and an adjoining plaza. Picasso's painting for the ballet *Three
Cornered Hat* provides a backdrop to the cool lobby off which
can be found the **Four Seasons** restaurant, designed by
Philip Johnson; as the name suggests, the interior decor
changes with the seasons.

The Empire State Building

Surely the most famous building in the world, the Empire State dominates the skyline and offers unparalleled views of Manhattan and beyond to those who take the elevator to its 86th and 102nd-floor observation decks. Located between 33rd and 34th Streets on 5th Avenue, it rises to a height of 1250 feet. Construction was a feat of architectural ingenuity and commenced at break-neck speed. At one point 14 storeys were added in just ten days, and 3,500 people were employed on the operation. It was completed in May 1931 at a cost of $45 million, $5 million under budget, when New York was in the depths of depression. Much of the building remained unlet until after World War II, and as a result the building was nicknamed the 'empty state'. On 28 July 1945 a B-25 bomber crashed into its 79th storey, killing 14 people. Another unwelcome visitor (of the celluloid type) was King Kong.

The skyscrapers seem to rush forward to populate the tip of the island as it sails out to sea, each one clamoring to be seen from afar, as if floating on the water.

Vincent Scully, art historian, *Architecture: The Natural and the Manmade*, 1991

The Twin Towers

The World Trade Center, built in 1970–76 in downtown Manhattan, is actually a series of interconnected modernist buildings of which the steel and glass twin towers are undoubtedly the most famous. 415m (1350ft) high, with 110 storeys, the towers are the highest buildings in New York and held the world record until pipped by the Sears Tower in Chicago. There is an observation deck on the top floor of Tower 2, which is open to the public and affords fantastic views. During the daytime the Center's 929,000m^2 (10 million^2 ft) of office space is home to around 50,000 workers. In February 1993 a terrorist bomb rocked the foundations of the Center killing five people.

NOTES

NOTES

MEMORABLE EVENTS

The Civil War Draft Riots

In the summer of 1863 New York witnessed its worst civil unrest ever. Between 13 and 16 July angry mobs of white, mainly Irish, immigrants rampaged through the city looting, burning and killing. They were enraged by the Republican government's introduction of compulsory conscription into the Union Army and a controversial get-out clause allowing those who could afford it to escape the draft. The earliest target was a draft office and later Republican property was attacked. The mob's resentment turned to black New Yorkers, many recently freed slaves whom they feared would compete for precious jobs. That afternoon the Colored Orphan Asylum on Fifth Avenue was sacked and burned and all over the city blacks and their sympathisers were attacked with astonishing brutality. Peace was finally restored on 15 and 16 July with the help of Union Army troops. The final death toll from the bloody three days was estimated at 105. Despite the opposition, around 110,000 volunteers enlisted during the course of the war.

Notes

NOTES

Great Blizzard

Between 12 and 14 March 1888 New York was smothered by a fierce blizzard that dumped around 52cm (21in) of snow on the city, blocking roads and highways and felling overground wires. In some places drifts reached up to the second floor of buildings and it was days before a thaw finally set in and New Yorkers could dig themselves out.

The blizzard remained the worst in the city's history until 1947 when, just after Christmas, almost 62cm (25in) fell. The winter of 1995–96 also proved long and harsh for New Yorkers. As snow piled up on the sidewalks the usually bustling streets and avenues fell eerily quiet and enterprising New Yorkers swished around town on skis.

NOTES

The Brooklyn Bridge Panic

New Yorkers waited for 13 years for the Brooklyn Bridge to be completed. The day it was officially opened, in May 1883, 150,000 people walked across it, marvelling at the enormous gothic arches that soared high over lower Manhattan and Brooklyn Heights, and at the web of steel cables and the magnificent views of the East River and city. The bridge remains a favourite place to stroll and admire the scenery.

Building the bridge was not without its difficulties, however. The designer, John Augustus Roebling, who invented wire cable, died just before work was to begin in 1869. His son, Washington Roebling, took over, but suffered from a crippling case of the bends and in a series of separate incidents a number of bridge workers lost their lives. There was further tragedy just days after the bridge opened on Memorial Day, 30 May, the day that commemorates the servicemen killed in American wars. A woman stumbled on the bridge, which was filled with sightseers, and as she screamed thousands pushed to see what was happening. In the commotion rumour spread that the bridge was collapsing and in the ensuing stampede to solid ground a dozen people were killed and many injured.

The Triangle Shirtwaist Factory Fire

At 4.30pm on 25 March, 1911, flames started to lick around bolts of fabric stored in the Triangle Shirtwaist Factory on the upper floors of a building on the corner of Washington Place and Greene Street. Less than an hour later the factory was gutted and 146 of the 500 women and girl seamstresses, mostly Jewish and Italian immigrants, were dead. In the panic many burned to death, unable to escape the building because the management had locked the doors to the stairwells to prevent the women stealing. Others fell to their deaths when a fire escape collapsed and still more chanced a leap from the ninth storey of the building. Their burning bodies littered the pavement below to the horror of onlookers. Had the owners seen fit to provide a sprinkler system, the escape routes not been locked and the fire service been able to stretch their ladders beyond the sixth floor of the building, the devastation and loss of life may not have been so bad. The fire, the worst factory fire in New York history, was a tragic lesson and following it new safety laws were enacted.

Notes

World's fairs

Three world's fairs have been held in New York – the first in 1853–4 contained displays of industrial and agricultural products, and artwork from around the world. The second in 1939–40 captured the nation's imagination with its themed zones – transportation, food, government, amusement, communications, production and distribution, and community interests. It was on this site in Flushing that the public had their first look at television, air conditioning (in a pavilion shaped like an igloo), nylon stockings and colour film. In one pavilion long distance phone calls could be made for nothing, in another Heinz gave away mountains of pickle-shaped brooches. At the 1964–5 fair IBM's basic computers were exhibited.

NEW YORK PEOPLE

Jimmy Durante

NOTES

Mrs Astor and Mrs Vanderbilt

Caroline Schermerhorn Astor, will forever be known as *The Mrs Astor*. In the late 19th century, using her impeccable credentials – old family, old money, educated in Paris, marriage to new money and pots of it – she became queen of New York society. Her annual balls were legendary, lavish affairs and anyone who had any social standing was invited.

Those who were included on Mrs Astor's invitation list knew that they had arrived. Undesirables were weeded out by her social secretary Ward McAllister, who was responsible for whittling down the list of New York's elite to the famous '400', ostensibly the number of people who could fit comfortably in Mrs Astor's magnificent ballroom. Ward McAllister explained that 'there are only about 400 people in fashionable New York society. If you go outside that number you strike people who are not at ease in a ballroom or else make other people not at ease.'

Not everyone was impressed. The writer Edith Wharton described it as 'a little "set" with its private catchwords, observances and amusements, and its indifference to anything outside its charmed circle'. Still, Mrs Astor had no rival, at least not until Alva Vanderbilt arrived on the scene. Alva, whose husband's wealth outstripped even William Astor's, was not on Mrs Astor's invitation list and Mrs Astor declined politely to receive her. Alva exacted her revenge in March

1883. She wanted to show off her new mansion, a chateau-like affair on Fifth Avenue, and decided that a huge fancy dress ball was in order. She proposed it for a Monday evening – Mrs Astor's opera night. Invitees were in a tizzy: the planning of costumes, said *The New York Times*, 'disturbed the sleep and occupied the waking hours of social butterflies, both male and female, for over six weeks'. Alva played by Mrs Astor's rules. She explained to Ward McAllister that it was with much regret that she could not invite Mrs Astor or her daughter, since she had never formally been introduced. Mrs Astor was forced to back down – her card was delivered to Alva's home and in return an invitation was issued.

The Vanderbilt Art Gallery

Martha Graham

When Martha Graham (1894–1991) arrived in New York from California in 1923 she danced in the traditional style of her teachers. Before long, however, she had developed an individual style based on minimalism and strongly influenced by her interest in religion and psychology. She popularized a new way of moving called Modern Dance, in which the body naturally expressed the feelings and the energy of the human condition. Whereas in traditional ballet, toes were pointed and backs ramrod straight, in this new dance feet often flexed and backs were contracted until every ounce of feeling was squeezed out and given shape.

During the 1930s she formed a women's dance company, and her early works of choreography were stark, taut and dramatic. She later opened a dance studio on **Fifth Avenue** between 12th and 13th Streets, and in 1938 invited Erick Hawkins to become the first male member of her company (they later married). Many members of Martha Graham's company, including Merce Cunningham, went on to become choreographers and dance company directors of renown.

NOTES

Malcolm X

Born Malcolm Little in 1925 in Omaha, Nebraska, Malcolm X moved in the 1940s, like hundreds of thousands of other young blacks, to the northeast in search of work. His was an eventful life — exciting, sometimes triumphant, and ultimately tragic. When he was six his father, a follower of black nationalist Marcus Garvey, was killed by whites. Later, while based in Boston but travelling regularly to New York, he became involved in drug dealing and petty crime. In 1946 he was jailed in Boston for theft and during his incarceration he discovered Islam and changed his name — the X represents his lost African ancestry. After his release in the early 1950s he joined the Nation of Islam and became the movement's best-known spokesman, a militant advocating separatism and denouncing non-violence. It was a line that put him at odds with others in the Civil Rights movement. After a pilgrimage to Mecca in 1964 he returned to New York, with slightly moderated views, and formed the Organisation of African-American Unity. A year later, while speaking at a political rally at the Audubon Ballroom on 165th Street, he was shot and fatally wounded. Lenox Avenue in Harlem is now called **Malcolm X Boulevard**.

Up and down and between Lenox and 7th and 8th Avenues, Harlem was like some technicolor bazaar. Hundreds of Negro soldiers and sailors, gawking and young like me, passed by … Every man without a woman on his arm was being 'worked' by the prostitutes. 'Baby, wanna have some fun?' the pimps would slide up close, stage-whispering, 'All kinds of women Jack – want a white woman?' And the hustlers were merchandising: 'Hundred dollar ring man, diamond, ninety dollar watch, too – look at 'em. Take 'em both for twenty-five.'

Malcolm X (1925–1965) describing his first visit to Harlem

Andy Warhol

> In the future everyone will be famous for fifteen
> minutes.
>
> Andy Warhol (1926–87)

Andy Warhol's Factory, a loft in 47th Street (which later moved to Union Square), was the hip place to be in the 1960s – anyone who was anyone was there: film makers, artists, musicians … the beautiful people. Warhol was an enigmatic character, born in 1931 in Pittsburgh to Polish parents, and originally a commercial artist. He became famous for his huge multicolour silk-screens of icons such as Marilyn Monroe, Jacqueline Kennedy and Elvis Presley. Many of his *avant garde* films were made at the Factory, including *Sleep* – just that, a guy sleeping – and *Kitchen*, which starred Edie Sedgwick, one of Warhol's 'superstars'. Another film, *Chelsea Girls*, documented the life of the demimonde in the **Chelsea Hotel**. In June 1968 uber-feminist Valerie Solanis, writer of the *Scum* (Society for Cutting Up Men) manifesto took the elevator up to the Factory, pulled out her .32 automatic pistol and fired three shots into Warhol. He survived that, but died in 1987 after routine gall bladder surgery.

Up-tight Rock 'n Roll, Whip Dancers, Film-
maker Freaks, Tapers, Anchovies, filming live
episodes of the 'Up-Tight' series
and including Film Premiere for the
first time anywhere: Andy Warhol's
MORE MILK YVETTE starring
Maria Montez and The Velvet
Underground.

   Advertisement for Warhol's Uptight
      shows, February 1966

NOTES

Donald Trump

Fred Trump may have been a real-estate developer in the outer boroughs of New York city but it is his son Donald whose name has become synonymous with real estate in the city today after his more than 20 years' wheeling and dealing of Manhattan's buildings and empty blocks. His glitzy high-rise complex **Trump Tower** on Fifth Avenue contains a shopping centre, apartments and the headquarters of his empire, which includes a number of luxurious apartment buildings and **The Plaza**, probably New York's most famous hotel. With the property slump at the end of the 1980s, Trump had to sell off a number of his assets, including an airline, but he has climbed back out of the doldrums and continues as one of the city's more flamboyant characters.

Joseph Papp

Synonymous with public theatre, Joseph Papp (1921–91) was responsible for introducing theatrical neighbourhood tours, and for bringing theatre to the people in the 1950s. His touring company has staged free performances of Shakespeare's works each summer from 1957 in **Central Park**.

Papp was committed to raising awareness of social issues and used his productions as a voice to speak for injustice and inequality. He used ticket receipts from the extremely popular *A Chorus Line* to sponsor less mainstream productions and support actors from minority groups.

Woody Allen

Woody Allen, born Allan Konigsberg in Brooklyn in 1935, has made a career out of being the archetypal angst-ridden New York Jew. After a stint as a stand-up comic, Allen turned his hand to plays and films, many of which are set in New York and are at least partly autobiographical, none more so than *Husbands and Wives*, in which he stars as a man who falls in love with someone young enough to be his daughter. Around the time of filming he had been embroiled in a highly public custody dispute after he had left long-time companion Mia Farrow for one of her adopted daughters. As well as movies, Allen is a keen clarinettist, and can be seen on Monday nights playing live at **Michael's Pub** on East 55th Street in midtown.

NOTES

Billie Holiday

One of the most important and influential jazz singers of her day, Billie Holiday (1915–59) began her singing career in **Harlem** in the early 1930s and started recording soon afterwards. Long-term contracts for **Café Society** in **Greenwich Village**, and prestigious performances at leading nightclubs earned Billie Holiday her reputation for evocative lyrics and expressive delivery. Throughout her career she fought racism denouncing inequality in her songs.

Leonard Bernstein

New York city provided composer and conductor Leonard Bernstein (1918–90) with inspiration for much of his work, not least for *West Side Story*, loosely based on the story of Shakespeare's *Romeo and Juliet*. The movie of the 1957 musical was filmed in the rundown streets of what was to later become the **Lincoln Center**, the performing arts complex that Bernstein had quite a hand in setting up. During his almost 50 year musical career, Bernstein, who lived for many years in the **Dakota** on West 72nd Street, conducted both the **New York City Symphony** and the **New York Philharmonic** orchestras, and with the Philharmonic, performed more concerts than any of his predecessors, who included Leopold Stokowski and Arturo Toscanini.

As well as *West Side Story*, Bernstein wrote a number of other works for the stage and concert hall including ballets, operas, symphonies, and orchestral, chamber and vocal works.

MUSIC, THEATRE, DANCE & ART

Creative New York

New York, a city where eccentricity is admired and new ideas applauded, has always proved an irresistible magnet for artists and performers, some of whom have gone on to become household names, while others have disappeared without trace. It is a place so full of variety and energy that it is virtually impossible not to be inspired in a creative way, a city where innovative and more traditional art, music and theatre can be seen in all sorts of settings from the world's grandest galleries and auditoriums to dusty workshops hidden away in non-descript office buildings.

> In every large city there will always be found a considerable number of persons who possess superior talents and information; and who, if not natives, are drawn to it by the peculiar encouragement which it holds out to their exertions ... New York has its share of persons sustaining this character.
>
> Timothy Dwight (1750–1817)

Concert Halls

> 'How do you get to Carnegie Hall?'
> 'Practice, practice, practice.'
> (old New York joke)

New Yorkers have an enormous appetite for classical music –
they lap it up on virtually every night, in everything from
concert halls to museums and neighbourhood churches. The
Renaissance-style **Carnegie Hall**, on West 57th Street, was
Manhattan's first great concert hall when it opened in 1891
with Tchaikovsky as guest conductor. For many years
Carnegie Hall was the home of the **New York Philharmonic**
before the orchestra moved to the **Avery Fisher Hall** at the
Lincoln Center. Also at the Lincoln Center is **Alice Tully
Hall**, a more intimate space than **Avery Fisher Hall**.

The Museum of Modern Art, the **Frick Collection**, **The
Cloisters** and the **Metropolitan Museum of Art** all host
classical and contemporary music performances on weekend
afternoons or evenings, while a number of old churches in
Manhattan provide wonderfully evocative settings for chamber
music concerts. A quick subway ride outside Manhattan, the
Brooklyn Academy of Music has, over the years, seen
performances by many of the world's greats, including Pablo
Casals and Sergei Rachmaninov, and continues to be one of
the city's top spots for classical and contemporary music.

Bargemusic, a cosy wood-panelled boat permanently moored next door to the renowned **River Café** in Brooklyn, offers a brilliant backdrop of lower Manhattan and a delicious spread of chocolate cake, wine and cheese along with first-rate classical concerts, played by professional musicians. Go on Thursday evenings and Sunday afternoons throughout the year for one of New York's best-kept secrets that even a lot of New Yorkers do not know about.

Lincoln Center

Administered by a non-profit making organisation, the Lincoln Center is the largest performing arts centre in America. President Eisenhower laid the first stone in 1959, and the many buildings were completed over the next decade.

Metropolitan Opera House

The centrepiece of the **Lincoln Center**, with its elaborate gold leaf, red carpets, marblework, crystal chandelier and enormous murals is a modern interpretation of a traditional opera house. Mocked for its conservative programme, it is similarly scorned for offering contemporary productions. Casts are international and productions lavish, but tickets are very expensive. It is the place to be seen both on stage and off.

New York State Theater

Home to the **New York City Opera**, the company has a reputation for dynamic productions with a contemporary and popular appeal. Performances range from *Madame Butterfly*, *South Pacific* to *The Pyjama Game*. Productions are mostly in English, with subtitles above the stage to help the audience understand the plot of foreign language productions. Cheaper ticket prices make performances more accessible.

The Theater has been the performance spot for the **New York City Ballet** since 1964.

Avery Fisher Hall

Originally the Philharmonic Hall, the **New York Philharmonic** moved here when it left **Carnegie Hall** in 1962. In July and August the hall becomes the annual home for the 'Mostly Mozart' series.

Alice Tully Hall

Alice Tully Hall boasts beautiful acoustics and is the place to hear recitals and chamber music. The hall is home to the **Chamber Music Society** and regular performances are held here by the students of the **Juilliard School of Music**.

Also here are the **Damrosch Park** and **Guggenheim Bandshell** providing open-air theatre throughout the summer, the **Vivian Beaumont Theater**, the **Library and Museum of the Performing Arts**, and the **Juilliard School of Music**.

NOTES

Tin Pan Alley

During the first half of the 20th century composers and music publishers grouped themselves together in what became known as Tin Pan Alley (an area that shifted over the years from 14th to 56th Streets with various stops on the way) and introduced a new way of aggressively marketing and publicising their latest material, advertising new sheet music in newspapers and employing musicians to play them in shops and on streets. The best-known songwriters in Tin Pan Alley included George M Cohan (*Give My Regards to Broadway*), Irving Berlin (*God Bless America*), George and Ira Gershwin (*Lady, Be Good!*) and Cole Porter (*Night and Day*). The advent of talking movies and the popularity of radio and **Broadway** brought their compositions to a huge audience. When Tin Pan Alley failed to keep up with the times in the 1950s and '60s, rock and roll, folk and country music became the pop music of the day, although the best-known songs of the Alley are still heard today.

Jazz

Harlem! How terribly Ray could hate it
sometimes, its brutality, gang rowdyism,
promiscuous thickness. Its hot desires. But, oh,
the rich blood-red color of it! The warm accent of
its composite voice, the fruitiness of its laughter,
the trailing rhythm of its 'blues' and the
improvised surprises of its jazz.

Claude McKay, *Home to Harlem*, 1928

The first recordings of Dixieland jazz were made in the city in
1917, and all types of jazz, from big band to Afro-Cuban,
have flourished, thanks to musicians such as Fats Waller,
Benny Goodman, Count Basie, Louis Armstrong, Dizzy
Gillespie and Duke Ellington (who wrote music in
the late 1920s for elaborate revues at the
Cotton Club). Jazz has had its ups and downs
over the years, but today musicians in clubs all
over the city continue to perform and revive all
styles of the music.

Musical theatre

Ask any visitor what they associate with New York and the response will invariably include theatre. The most widely known New York theatre has got to be the **Broadway** musical. Musical theatre originated as a unique combination of European operetta, vaudeville and burlesque and the American minstrel show. The great names include George and Ira Gershwin, who wrote the music and lyrics for *Girl Crazy*, amongst many others.

Also at the top of the list is the famous team Rogers and Hammerstein, who gave us such American classics as *Oklahoma*, *Carousel*, *South Pacific*, *The King and I*, and *The Sound of Music* in the '40s '50s and '60s. All of these have had successful periodic revivals. Leonard Bernstein took the classical theme of *Romeo and Juliet* and with librettist Arthur Laurents, lyricist Stephen Sondheim and director Jerome Robbins created the immortal *West Side Story*. At the end of the '60s the musical *Hair* was an important milestone bringing contemporary rock music and nudity to the popular stage. Stephen Sondheim set new trends in the '70s with *Company, A Little Night Music,* and *Sweeney Todd* among others and Bob Fossey created the record-setting *A Chorus Line*. Today there are many British imports such as *Cats, Les Miserables*, and *Phantom of the Opera*.

Notes.

Experimental music

Modern experimental music also made its mark in New York. John Cage (1912–92), much of whose work was influenced by Eastern philosophies, created compositions for anything but traditional instruments, favouring instead such items as toy pianos, plants, blenders and radios. One 1952 piece, *4' 33"*, is even made up only of odd sounds heard in the theatre, while the performers on stage remain absolutely silent. Cage also collaborated with choreographer Merce Cunningham and scored several compositions for his dance group.

In the '60s Philip Glass started performing his minimalist works in museums and art galleries around the city, and although today he has a wide audience for his music, his opera *Einstein on the Beach*, a collaboration with performance artist Robert Wilson, startled audiences when it was first performed at the **Metropolitan Opera House** in 1976.

Rap

A particularly urban style of music developed in the **Bronx** in the 1970s – rap, a form closely associated with black residents of the city and one that evolved at the same time as the highly acrobatic break dancing. Rap was originally performed live, using inexpensive resources – several turntables at once providing a backing for the performers to chant their rhyming verses – but has eventually become a highly sophisticated and commercially popular form of music across the country.

NOTES

Drama

Since 1750 when audiences flocked to see an English touring company performance of *Richard III*, theatre has been widely supported by New York audiences. In the early part of this century, the work of non-American realist dramatists such as Ibsen, Shaw, Chekhov, and Pirandello gained wide audiences. By the 1930s and '40s plays by native playwrights such as George Hoffman, Maxwell Anderson and Eugene O'Neill were heralding a new era of psychological drama. African-American writers such as James Baldwin and Lorraine Hansbury were staged to great acclaim. The Public Theater and Joseph Papp helped to fire a public appetite for new drama. Later years saw the popularity of the works of Tennessee Williams, and by the 1960s Edward Albee and Arthur Miller gained an international audience. Today it is possible to see many new works and classic revivals in theatres scattered throughout the city.

NOTES

Performance art

A very, very New York thing, performance art emerged in the 1970s and has made its mark in an international arts scene. This new art form which combined many aspects of the performing and plastic arts challenged all previous views of art and addressed the big questions, What is art? and Who is the audience? Performances took place (and continue to) all over the city from small shows in SoHo and TriBeCa, to river barges in the Hudson, to the Port Authority Bus Terminal, to large concert halls. Dancers, artists, writers, musicians, film and video makers have forged new ways of working together to make new art for the new times. Performers such as Yvonne Rainer and Tricia Brown developed a new vocabulary for dance made up of every day gestures while Laurie Anderson and Meredith Monk pioneered important works using sound and movement. Performance art can be seen any day or night of the week.

Ballet

Ballet in New York is synonymous with Russian-born choreographer and teacher George Balanchine (1904–83), and art patron Lincoln Kirstein. At the latter's invitation Balanchine came to New York in 1932 where along with Kirstein he formed the **New York City Ballet** in 1948, which is known today as one of the greatest classical ballet companies around. The **American Ballet Theater** is equally impressive and one can see both companies performing regularly at the **Lincoln Center**. For a glorious international ballet experience catch the Bolshoi or the Paris Opera Ballet at the **Met**. Other exciting and sometimes unconventional performances can be enjoyed at the **Brooklyn Academy of Music** or the **City Centre of Music and Drama**.

NOTES

Modern dance

After Martha Graham's pioneering work in the 1930s, modern dance took a more abstract direction after the War with the works of choreographers/dancers Alwin Nickolais, Merce Cunningham and Paul Taylor, all of whom formed their own internationally known companies. Alvin Ailey offered new works based on African-American themes and struggles, often accompanied by haunting spirituals. In the 1960s a group of post-modern choreographers formed a co-operative known as the Judson Church School, working to develop non-traditional techniques and chance juxtapositions often incorporating non-trained dancers. This led to the '70s experimental work of Meredith Monk, Dan Waggoner, Remy Charlip (also well-known as a painter and author of over 30 remarkably successful children's titles including the inspiring *Arm in Arm*) and Twyla Tharp (who became mainstream with her choreography for her movie version of *Hair*). In the '80s Mark Morris experimented with a new movement vocabulary for opera while others like Bill T Jones and Arnie Zane linked movement with contemporary art and culture.

A wide variety of dance can be seen at the **92nd Street Y**, the **Merce Cunningham Studio**, the **Dance Theater Workshop**, **The Kitchen**, **PS122**, **The Manhattan City Center** and the **Brooklyn Academy of Music**.

Contemporary dance

The **Joyce Theatre** in Chelsea is the main spot for all types of contemporary dance, including Spanish and jazz dance. At the other end of Manhattan, the **Dance Theater of Harlem**, famous for its ethnic, traditional and modern productions, has its home.

For an utterly New York experience, in a setting that matches the razzle-dazzle of the show, it is hard to go past the **Radio City Music Hall** spectaculars, featuring the high kicks and glitz of the Rockettes.

Modern art

Along with top-class galleries such as the **Museum of Modern Art** and the **Guggenheim**, New York also has a thriving and well-established artists' community – its members come from all over the world to be part of it. Such big names as Marcel Duchamp and Piet Mondrian settled in the city, inspired by its concentrated vigour.

During the 20th century various artistic movements developed in Manhattan, most notably abstract expressionism – practised for some time by Jasper Johns – and later pop art. Major players in this movement include Andy Warhol, Roy Lichtenstein and Robert Rauschenberg.

Private art galleries are scattered all over the city, particularly **SoHo**, the **Upper East Side** and **57th Street**, but while SoHo, with cheap rents and large loft spaces, was a centre for artists in the '60s and '70s, soaring rents have now forced all but the most successful to move out of the area. Many have tried to re-create SoHo in the industrial area of **Williamsburg**, Brooklyn.

NOTES

LITERARY ADDRESSES

Literature

New York has always been a literary magnet with writers, poets, playwrights and journalists contributing to a national literature. From the Knickerbocker writers of the 1820s inspired by Washington Irving (*The Sketch Book of Geoffrey Crayon, Gent.*, 1819–20, which included 'Rip van Winkle') and James Fenimore Cooper (*The Last of the Mohicans*, 1826) to Horace Creeley's first newspaper *The New York Tribune*, to Allen Ginsberg's Beat poetry of the 1950s, and work of F Scott Fitzgerald and Hemingway, New York has been the literary heart of America.

Many national journals and magazines began publication in New York including *Vanity Fair* and *The New Yorker*. *The Little Review* published James Joyce's *Ulysses* in installments from 1918–1920, when none of the big publishing companies would touch the work. The absolute contrasts and vibrancy of New York have always inspired authors. Writers such as Edith Wharton wrote of New York's Gilded Age in *The Age of Innocence* (1920), while Fitzgerald wrote the romantic *This Side of Paradise* (1920) and the satiric *The Great Gatsby* (1925).

The energy of the 1930s inspired Dashiell Hammett to write *The Maltese Falcon* (1930) and Lillian Hellman wrote *The Children's Hour* (1934) and *The Little Foxes* (1939). Tennessee Williams in the '40s and '50s wrote *The Glass*

Menagerie (1945), while William Styron finished *Lie Down in Darkness* (1951). Columbia University emerged as a hot bed of poetic talent and literary criticism with such students as John Berryman and Jack Kerouac.

After the War years New York raced ahead becoming home to many of the great American talents, all of whom helped to create a contemporary national style. This included luminaries such as Norman Mailer, John Updike, Phillip Roth, Saul Bellow, William Burrows, and Truman Capote.

In this century African-American writers found their voice and cultivated a wide audience. Writers such as LeRoi Jones, Ishmael Reed and Nikki Giovanni gathered in New York and helped to create a distinctive strand of American literature. Mary McCarthy's novel *The Group* (1963) offered a popular and somewhat biting view of Upper West Side life and morals. In recent years Tom Wolfe's *The Bonfire of the Vanities* (1987) explored the fairytale decadence of the world of New York high finance and power.

Washington Irving

NOTES

7 Middagh Street

With its leafy streets, old brownstone houses and views across the East River to Manhattan, Brooklyn Heights has long been a desirable neighbourhood, and particularly so with artists and writers. Some of the Heights' most well-known residents have included Arthur Miller, Norman Mailer, Tennessee Williams and Truman Capote. An almost communal living arrangement was set up at the brownstone 7 Middagh Street (since demolished to make way for an expressway) in the 1940s, with poet W H Auden being housemaster of such creative talent as stripper Gipsy Rose Lee, who finished her mystery, *The G-String Murders*, there; Paul Bowles, author of *The Sheltering Sky*, and his wife, writer Jane Bowles, who lived on the second floor; composer Benjamin Britten, who hammered away at the piano in the parlour, and neurotic author Carson McCullers, who wrote her first (and very successful) novel *The Heart is a Lonely Hunter*, when she was 23.

Grove Court

Once anybody who was anybody would only live in a house with a street frontage. Grove Court, a row of six houses tucked between two buildings on Grove Street, was totally undesirable, suitable for the working classes when it was built in the 1850s. Now its out-of-the-way location has helped make it one of the Village's most exclusive addresses.

> In a little district west of Washington Square
> [Grove Court] the streets have run crazy and
> broken themselves into small strips called 'places'.
> These 'places' make strange angles and curves.
> One street crosses itself a time or two. An artist
> once discovered a valuable possibility in this street.
> Suppose a collector with a bill for paints, paper
> and canvas should, in traversing this route,
> suddenly meet himself coming back, without a
> cent having been paid on account!
> O Henry, *The Last Leaf*, 1902

The Algonquin

> ... the Round Table was just a lot of people telling
> jokes and telling each other how good they were.
>> Dorothy Parker (1893–1967)

> Dammit, it was the twenties and we had to be
> smarty.
>> Dorothy Parker

The queen of the sharp tongue, Dorothy Parker, was sacked
from her position as writer at *Vanity Fair* in 1920 for writing
mean reviews of three major plays. She gained quite a
following for her wry book reviews, but will always be
associated with her membership of the Algonquin Round
Table, a group of literary and theatrical figures, journalists
and critics. It included Alexander Woollcott from *The New
York Times*, Harold Ross, who founded *The New Yorker*,
humourist Robert Benchley and writer Franklin Adams, with
occasional visits from actors Harpo Marx and Tallulah
Bankhead. The members became the glamorous and witty
people the public liked to read about.

The Cooper Union Building

Standing on the island of **Cooper Square** in the East Village is a great hulk of a building dedicated to free speech and education. Founded in 1859 by philanthropist and reformer Peter Cooper, the Cooper Union was initially formed to provide higher education for the working class, but has also since the end of the 19th century offered art and architecture courses. Public debates and lectures have been held constantly at the Cooper Union – Abraham Lincoln bowled New Yorkers over in 1860 with his 'might is right' speech in which he criticised the pro-slavery policies of the southern states; other famous lecturers have included Mark Twain, Harriet Beecher Stowe and Russian writer Maxim Gorky, who was not welcome elsewhere in the city because of his Bolshevik views.

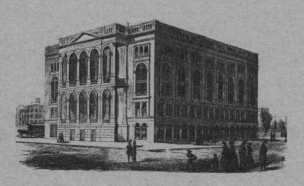

THE BUSINESS OF
NEW YORK

Fashion

New York established itself as the American fashion capital in the early 19th century, with custom-made clothing dominating the industry until the mass production of 'ready-to-wear' was introduced around the 1850s. In the 1890s a distinctly American style emerged in the form of the sporty and natural 'Gibson girl', who was a world away from her more formal Paris cousin. New York has grown steadily as a fashion capital over the years, but had a huge growth spurt during World War II, when the country was cut off from the influence of Paris. In those days the industry was centred around Fifth Avenue and 57th Street, but is now found on **Seventh Avenue**. The pavements are crowded with armies of men pushing racks of clothes from one spot to another, and passers-by are handed reams of flyers advertising workshop sales. Twice a year, **Bryant Park**, behind **New York Public Library**, becomes the city's fashion centre as giant tents are set up for all the major American designers to hold shows of their next season's creations.

The diamond industry

The diamond business had always been important in New York, but started becoming even more so when diamond traders, mainly orthodox Jews, fled to the East Coast when Hitler invaded Belgium and Holland during World War II. Previously the industry had been clustered around Canal Street and Fulton Street, but many of the newcomers set up shop on West 47th Street, between Fifth and Sixth Avenues, where the business, including offices, retail stores, workshops and secondhand jewellery shops, is based today. Transactions in the area are finalised with a handshake and the words 'mazel und brucha' (luck and blessing).

NOTES

Finance

> ...the Rome, the Paris, the London of the
> twentieth century, the city of ambition, the dense
> magnetic rock, the irresistible destination of all
> those who insist on being where things are
> happening – and he was among the victors.
> Tom Wolfe, *The Bonfire of the Vanities*, 1987

Wall Street, in lower Manhattan, literally once had a wooden wall, built in 1653 from one side of the island to the other to keep marauding Indians and British troops away from the Dutch town. It was never needed, which was just as well as the planks proved irresistible to local home owners as firewood. Today the name of the one third of a mile long street is synonymous with wealth and power.

Its birth as a major financial centre happened in 1792 when 24 brokers who had traded at 68 Wall Street decided only to deal with each other, and thus the **New York Stock Exchange** was founded. As with any financial institution, the New York Stock Exchange has had its ups and downs, most spectacularly on 29 October 1929, when the market crashed, signalling the start of the Great Depression.

Flowers

The flower district, just a few blocks south of **Macy's**, is one of those areas of New York that appears without warning; a welcome patch of greenery and colour in the otherwise dull area around Sixth Avenue and West 28th Street. Many of the shops are wholesale, so not much is for sale to the public, but that does not stop New Yorkers from snaking their way through virtually full-size trees that have crept out onto the pavement, and stopping to smell the roses – or whatever else happens to be in bloom.

Theatres used to be clustered in this area before moving up around **Broadway** in the 1940s; West 28th Street was the original Tin Pan Alley, where music publishers sold songs to artists and nearby theatre producers.

Publishing

The first magazines in New York were published in the 1750s, and by 1880 the city produced two thirds of the major US magazines. As industries such as fashion emerged in the city, so too did magazines like *Harper's Bazaar* and *Vogue*. The 1920s saw the birth of three important magazines – *Reader's Digest*, which was founded in a basement in Greenwich Village in 1922; the news magazine *Time*, started in 1923 by Henry Luce and Briton Haddon; and *The New Yorker*, which began as a humorous magazine in 1925 but eventually took on a literary slant. Over the years New York magazines have assumed different personalities, most notably *Cosmopolitan*, which started as a news and political magazine in 1887 – hard to imagine looking at the magazine today after it was given a major facelift and a sex change by Helen Gurley Brown in 1965.

New York has also been a major world centre for book publishing – the first book was published in the city in the 1690s. Over the years companies have sprung up and flourished. Some of the well-known ones to have started in New York include Random House, Golden Books, Henry Holt and Doubleday. In recent years, many of the publishing companies have been taken over by huge conglomerates.

CRIMES & SCANDALS

NOTES

William 'Boss' Tweed

A scoundrel of the first order, William 'Boss' Tweed was a man whose physical proportions equalled his mighty political clout. Along with his political cronies, known as the Tweed Ring, he filched up to $200 million from city funds over his 20-year career in New York City politics, all the while shrewdly keeping his popular appeal by calling for the building of schools, orphanages and the like. Unlikely sums were recorded, such as $10,000 spent in a small city office on stationery in a month. But in 1871 his bubble burst and he was toppled from office. It must have taken Tweed by surprise since only months before he was arrested he found out about a proposed statue of him and said: 'Statues are not erected to living men. I claim to be a live man and hope (Divine Providence permitting) to survive in all my vigour politically and physically, some years to come.' Fate intended otherwise.

Tweed's downfall, precipitated by reports in the press, coincided with the the completion of the New York City Courthouse in Chambers Street, which was started in 1861 with a budget of $250,000, and eventually finished a decade later with a final bill of almost $13 million. Tweed and his ring were reckoned to have embezzled around two thirds of that figure through kickbacks from contractors.

Tweed was jailed on Roosevelt Island where, much to the consternation of *Harper's* magazine and others, he was kept in relative comfort in well-furnished lodgings, while a 'friendless convict' endured long hours in his spartan cell. He could entertain friends, stroll around the grounds of the island and keep up with his correspondence through his private secretary. In 1875 he escaped after a family visit, making his way, via Cuba, to Spain. His freedom was short lived and he was quickly identified and returned to New York where he languished in prison until his death in 1878. He is buried in Green Wood Cemetery and his name lives on in Chambers Street where the courthouse, now municipal offices, is known as the **Tweed Courthouse**.

NOTES

The Rosenbergs

It was a family affair for Ethel and Julius Rosenberg and his brother-in-law David Greenglass, an employee at the atomic station at Los Alamos, New Mexico; all were accused by the FBI of being part of a New York spy ring committed to sending atomic secrets to the Soviet Union. Julius Rosenberg, a dedicated communist, had worked for the US Signal Corps during World War II, and it was then that he allegedly transmitted the information. To avoid the death sentence, Greenglass testified against the Rosenbergs, who became the first – and so far, only – married couple to be executed in New York State when they went to the electric chair at Sing Sing Prison on 19 June 1953.

Son of Sam

Boston had its strangler, and in the mid 1970s New York unwillingly had David Berkowitz, also known as Son of Sam, a postman who was convicted of shooting to death, in one year, five women and one man, apparently selecting his female victims after spotting them in parked cars with their male companions. He left a note signed 'Son of Sam' at each crime scene, and to gain publicity wrote to newspapers, blaming both demons and a mystery man called Sam for the shootings. New Yorkers could finally sleep easy again when Berkowitz was caught in August 1977, partly trapped by a parking ticket he received on the night of his last killing. He willingly acknowledged the murders and was sentenced to 30 years in prison. In 1991 the US Supreme Court passed the Son of Sam law, limiting the ability of convicted criminals to earn money from talking or writing about their crimes.

Sydney Biddle Barrows

Prostitution has been part of New York life since English and Dutch women of the night plied their wares along the Battery waterfront in the late 17th century. Various parts of the city have been red light districts over the years, including SoHo in the middle of the 19th century and Union Square towards the end of the 1800s.

Prostitution moved uptown – and onto the front page of the tabloids – when it was discovered that the brothel Cachet, at 307 West 74th Street, was run by socialite Sydney Biddle Barrows, dubbed the Mayflower Madame by the newspapers because two of her ancestors were original settlers of the Plymouth Colony. She was arrested in 1984, but cashed in on her notoriety by becoming a regular on the TV talk show circuit proffering advice on how to be irresistible in bed.

NOTES

Bernhard Goetz

To some he was a hero, to others he went too far, but to all New Yorkers electrical engineer Bernhard Goetz will always be known as the Subway Vigilante after using an unlicensed handgun to shoot four black youths who had asked him for money on the No 2 subway near Chambers Street station on 22 December 1984. He was acquitted of attempted murder in a 1987 trial, but sentenced to a year in prison for carrying the gun. One of the youths was paralysed and brain damaged in the shooting; the others recovered. After serving eight months at Rikers Island, Goetz quietly moved back into his apartment and now earns his living repairing electrical equipment.

Leona Helmsley

Dubbed the 'Queen of Mean' for her abrasive personality and harsh treatment of staff, Leona Helmsley will go down in the record books for her philosophy that 'Only the little people pay taxes.' This hotel and real estate mogul (she and husband Harry bought and renovated 21 hotels in New York, including the sumptuous **Helmsley Palace Hotel**) was charged with tax evasion in 1988. She was sent to prison for four years after being convicted of dodging more than $1 million in back taxes. Her husband, declared unfit to stand trial, stayed at home waiting for her.

According to cellmates Leona kept her crown on during her incarceration by bossing other prisoners around and ordering them to do her washing, cleaning and bed-making for her.

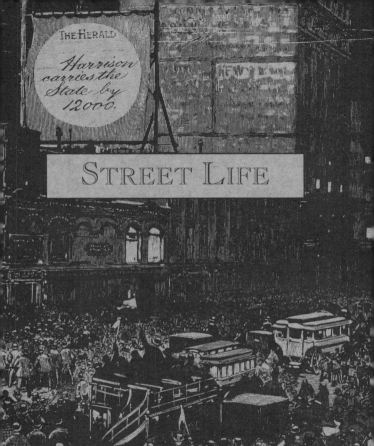

THE.HERALD

*Harrison
carries the
State by
12000.*

STREET LIFE

Broadway

> What hurrying human tides, or day or night!
> What passions, winnings, losses, ardors, swim thy
> waters!
>
> Walt Whitman (1819–92) *Broadway*

Broadway runs for 27km (17 miles) through the Island of
Manhattan, defying the grid system and cutting through
neighbourhoods as diverse as the financial district and
Harlem. Originally an Indian trail, it was named Heere
Straat or High Street by the Dutch and later became
synonymous with New York theatre. It has always been a
bustling thoroughfare: one observer noted in 1807 that
Broadway above Wall Street was 'lined with large
commodious shops of every description, well stocked with
European and Indian goods, and exhibiting as splendid and
varied a show in their windows as can be met in London'.

At the intersection of Broadway and Seventh Avenue is
Times Square, the focal point for Broadway's theatreland and
venue for riotous New Year's celebrations. News headlines
flash around an electronic billboard at No.1 Times Square.

NOTES

Bleecker Street

> Here [in Greenwich Village] a woman could say
> damn right out loud and still be respected.
>
> Art Young, *On My Way*, 1928

A dogleg of a street that changes personality block by block, Bleecker Street starts its journey on the Bowery at **CBGB's**, the music venue, and heads west. After running past New York University residential buildings, Bleecker Street becomes a strip of bars and music dives before hitting the corner of McDougal Street, the site of **Cafe Figaro**, a favourite haunt of the Beat poets during the '60s. At Sixth Avenue, Bleecker Street heads northwest and turning into a mini-Little Italy for a few blocks, but then as the street meanders towards its westerly end at Eighth Avenue, it becomes quieter and more sedate, with bookshops, unusual giftshops, small neighbourhood restaurants and elegant antique shops.

Columbus Avenue

New York neighbourhoods are expected to change their personalities every 20 years or so as whole new waves of residents move into the area and buildings become gentrified or run down, or changed from commercial to residential use. One block west of Central Park, Columbus Avenue of Manhattan's Upper West Side has not so much changed its personality since the area was transformed from a working-class district into a haven for young professionals in the past few decades, but does regularly try on a new wardrobe of clothes, with new cafés, restaurants and boutiques springing up all the time, and disappearing just as quickly. It is a good place for browsing, or for relaxing and people-watching from one of the many outdoor eateries slung along the street. Many of the side-streets of Columbus Avenue are worth a diversion, with elegant brownstones and apartment buildings.

Mulberry Street

Italians have been in Mulberry Street since the 1850s and today the street and those adjacent still exude an old-world charm despite the fact that Chinatown is gatecrashing from all sides. This is the place to buy homemade mozzarella, sausages and fresh pasta and to indulge in delicious cappuccino and little cakes in one of the sidewalk cafes. **Ferrara's** on Grand Street is a favourite place. In the evening Little Italy bustles with strollers, and diners spill out onto the sidewalks in summer. One restaurant, **Umberto's Clam House**, became infamous when mobster Joey Gallo was shot and killed during a family dinner in 1972. It closed in December 1996.

Little Italy is at its most vibrant in September when the **San Gennaro** festival takes over Mulberry Street. An effigy of the patron saint of Naples is paraded around the streets between food stalls and palm readers.

Canal Street

Canal Street is the bustling main artery of Chinatown whose population has grown from 150 in 1859 to around 70,000 today. Business activity is centred here, spilling over into Mott Street, and it is a haven for bargain hunters whether they are looking for a cheap watch, or a quick meal at one of the many restaurants in the area. Food stores sell an unimaginable variety of exotic fruits and vegetables, curious shellfish and squabbling crabs that are loaded into paper bags.

NOTES

Parks & Gardens

NOTES

Central Park

When New Yorkers want to get away from New York without leaving it, it is a short hop to Central Park, which is not a park in the formal sense but more a Disneyland-like re-creation of nature, starting at 59th Street in the middle of Manhattan. The park had an inauspicious start before landscape architects transformed it in 1858. It took almost 20 years to create, half a million trees were planted, almost 96km (60 miles) of paths laid, several lakes and a number of ponds made, and four roads excavated and sunk below grass level. Now it is the spot for everything from watching birds or Shakespeare's plays to rollerblading and model-yacht sailing. Today, one of the park's most visited, and yet most peaceful areas, is **Strawberry Fields**, created on the West Side around 72nd Street in memory of murdered Beatle John Lennon.

In spite of its rockwork grottoes and tunnels, its pavilions and statues, its too numerous paths and pavements, lakes too big for the landscape and bridges too big for the lakes, [Central Park] expresses all the fragrance and freshness of the most charming moment of the year …

Henry James, *The Bostonians*, 1886

New York Botanical Gardens

With the financial help of such businessmen as Cornelius Vanderbilt, Andrew Carnegie and J P Morgan, the New York Botanical Gardens was developed in the 1890s on land at the northern end of Bronx Park. Over the years the collection of plants and trees has become a veritable United Nations of the flora world, with many of the more delicate and exotic housed in the **Enid A Haupt Conservatory**, which is made up of eleven fanciful domed glass and iron pavilions. For gardeners and ecologists the grand-scale garden displays include a fern forest, a palm court where a quarter of all species are cultivated, a garden forest, rock garden, rose garden, a desert garden and the **Jane Watson Irwin Perennial Garden**.

Gramercy Park

Reminiscent of some of London's exclusive squares, Gramercy Park, at the south end of Lexington Avenue, is empty most of the day since it is New York's only private park, open solely to residents of the area who are lucky enough to hold keys. A pretty focus of the neighbourhood, the park was built in the 1830s on reclaimed swampland and is now surrounded by some spectacular buildings, including, on the west side, two houses with New Orleans-type cast-iron porches and the **National Arts Club** on the south side.

Union Square Greenmarket

Even if you are not in the market for buying, Union Square
Greenmarket, held rain, hail or snow on Wednesdays, Fridays
and Saturdays, is a whiff of country in the city and a terrific
place to see New Yorkers going about their daily business,
sampling herbed goat cheese, buying armsful of hedgerow
flowers or drinking cups of fresh apple cider. Farmers, bakers,
fishermen, flowergrowers, cheesemakers and winemakers
travel into Manhattan from the surrounding countryside with
their produce – all seasonal, locally grown and locally made –
a pineapple will never be seen at the Greenmarket, nor a
turnip sold in summer.

IBM Building

While some cities are dotted with small parks, New York is peppered with secret gardens, splashes of green in unexpected places to be enjoyed year round. One of the most dramatic is the courtyard of the IBM Building, built in 1983 between East 56th and 57th Streets near Madison Avenue. This soaring greenhouse landscaped with massive clumps of bamboo, and even a small café in one corner is a restful retreat when Arctic winds are howling outside.

SIGHTS

Washington Square Arch

Fifth Avenue was shining in the sun when they
left the Brevoort and started walking toward
Washington Square.

Irwin Shaw, *Girls in Their Summer Dresses*

For six years before Washington Square Arch was built in
1895 to commemorate the inauguration of George
Washington, a temporary wooden arch stood in its place.
Both were designed by Stanford White, an architect
responsible for grand townhouses, clubs, statues and public
buildings around the city. But all is not as it seems in the
solid-looking structure that stands at the southern end of
Fifth Avenue. It is, in fact, hollow – above the arch itself is
a little room lit by skylights and reached by a winding
staircase in the western leg. In 1917 six rebelrousers stopped
in the room on their way to the roof, where they proclaimed
the **Greenwich Village** a republic.

Nor is all as it seems in the 24,000m² (9½ acres) of
Washington Square, a mecca for buskers, protesters,
students from the nearby New York University and Villagers
after a breath of fresh air. In the late 18th century the square
was used as a cemetery for victims of a cholera outbreak, and
the northwest corner was the site of public hangings.

Pierpont Morgan Library

Described by the *The Times* (London) as 'probably the greatest collector of things splendid and beautiful and rare who has ever lived', J Pierpont Morgan Sr built a library to house his priceless collection of manuscripts and prints. This exquisite neo-Renaissance style building by architect Charles Follen McKim was built in 1906 at a cost of $1,150,000.

The collection containing Rembrandts, Mahler manuscripts, rare books and prints, including a Gutenberg bible, work by Kate Greenaway, John Tenniel's illustrations of Lewis Carroll's *Alice in Wonderland*, and original manuscript leaves of one of Mozart's *horn concertos* was opened to an appreciative public in 1924 by his son J Pierpont Morgan Jr.

The name of Pierpont Morgan was first and foremost synonymous with the world of high finance. The financial trust which he established and took his name served the most influential of New Yorker's elite families and on three occasions saved the city from bankruptcy.

NOTES

The New Colossus

Give me your tired, your poor,
Your huddled masses yearning to breathe free
The wretched refuse of your teeming shore.
Send these, the homeless, tempest-tost to me,
I lift my lamp beside the golden door.

Emma Lazarus (1849–87) engraved on the
base of the Statue of Liberty

Statue of Liberty

The Statue of Liberty was a gift from the French to the people of America and, for those sailing into New York's harbour after she was erected in 1886, she was a symbol of hope and freedom. Liberty was designed by Frédéric-Auguste Bartholdi, and one Alexandre Gustave Eiffel, later famed for his tower, worked on the iron framework. The Statue of Liberty, the world's largest metal statue, stands 120m (395ft) high above New York's harbour. Its copper skin is a mere 2.4mm (3/32in) thick and it is a breathless 354 steps to the top of the crown. New Yorkers came out in force on 4 July 1986 to celebrate the restoration and 100th anniversary of the statue.

Notes

Little Church around the Corner

This little slip of a church, which dates from 1849 and has a small, tranquil garden, earned its name after the minister of another nearby and more fashionable church refused to bury actor George Holland and suggested that 'the little church around the corner' might be happy to fulfil the lowly task. Holland's friend, another actor, Joseph Jefferson, replied, 'God bless the little church around the corner', and the name stuck. His words are now commemorated in one of the stained-glass windows of the church, which also contains a memorial to the actress Gertrude Lawrence, who died in 1952, and glass windows honouring actors Edwin Booth and Mary Shaw.

Cathedral of St John the Divine

Work was begun on this colossal cathedral in 1892 and continues today. When the building is finished it will be the largest cathedral in the world. In 1911 the French Gothic designs of Ralph Adams Cram were adopted but work ceased in 1942 after his death and did not resume until 1979. At that stage only the huge nave and west front of the building, but not the towers and transepts, had been completed.

Up until 1992 local stonecutters, using traditional stone-carving techniques, worked on the cathedral. Today most work has ceased because of lack of funds and it will be many decades before it is finished. Some of the stonework detail is marvellous – especially the New York skyline that has been chiselled out of the top of one of the columns.

St Patrick's Cathedral

The largest Catholic cathedral in America was begun in 1850 on a site that was originally intended as a graveyard. Archbishop John Hughes was scorned for his ambition in opting for a cathedral rather than a church, more so because the cost of building was way beyond the city's limits. The result, designed by architect James Renwick is one of the best examples of Gothic Revival in New York. The interior, with bronze statues and huge stained glass windows provides an amazing backdrop in which to listen to concerts.

Rockefeller Center

Along with the **Empire State Building** and the **Statue of Liberty**, Rockefeller Center, which runs between Fifth and Sixth Avenues between 48th and 51st Street, must be one of New York's most recognised landmarks, not least for the skating rink. In summer the rink turns into an outdoor eating area, watched over by the golden Prometheus, and usually a swarm of tourists and shoppers. The complex, built between 1932 and 1940 by John D Rockefeller, son of the oil magnate, is possibly the best large-scale urban development anywhere, incorporating shops, restaurants (the most famous being **The Rainbow Room**), rooftop gardens, theatres and plenty of landscaped outdoor space between the buildings. As beautiful as the exteriors of the buildings are, with their Art Deco detailing, the lobbies of many are worth checking out for their dramatic artwork.

NOTES

Grand Central Station

As a bullet seeks its target, shining rails in every
part of our great country are aimed at Grand
Central Station, heart of the nation's greatest city.
Opening of Grand Central Station, broadcast over the
NBC Radio Blue Network, starting 1937

Even though the railway has lost most of its business to the
airlines and long-distance Amtrak trains use **Penn Station**,
Grand Central Station, used by half a million suburban
commuters daily, is still one of the city's great landmarks.
The first **Grand Central Depot** was built on East 42nd

Street by Cornelius Vanderbilt in 1871. With the introduction of electric trains in the early 1900s, the railways decided to build the present terminal, a spectacular Beaux Arts structure housing shops, restaurants (including the famed **Oyster Bar**) and 48 pairs of rail tracks, completing construction in 1913.

The station almost suffered a terrible indignity in the 1970s when a developer planned to plonk a tower block on top of it, but conservationists, led by Jacqueline Kennedy Onassis, came to the rescue, helping to preserve the building in all its classical glory.

South Street Seaport

from **Manhattan** in **Leaves of Grass**
City of hurried and sparkling water! city of spires
  and masts!
City nested in bays! my city!
           Walt Whitman, 1860

In the days when ships were the main form of international
travel, Manhattan was ringed by working wharves. Today
many have been demolished, turned into sporting complexes
or, as in the case of South Street Seaport on the east side of
lower Manhattan, a museum-plus-shopping centre. Much of
the seaport, with its cobbled streets and quaint buildings, has
remained virtually intact. Wandering through the area at
dusk, out of peak time, can be an eerie experience. Piers are
lined with old sailing vessels and sunset views from the top of
the newly built **Pier 17** are breathtaking.

Jed's entrance into New York was magnificent. He came swooping down out of the noisy sunlight. His ears were full of the hoot of tugs and the crying of gulls. His eyes were dazzled with the tall buildings that rose, sparkling with windows like mica, to meet him as the liner nosed into the harbor. Walking down the gangplank, briefcase under his arm, he squinted through the glare to try to make out the faces scattered like spilled peas in the shadow of the pier below.

John Dos Passos, *Most Likely to Succeed*, 1954

Shopping

Taking up a whole city block at West 34th Street, **Macy's** calls itself the biggest department store in the world and stocks everything from packets of biscuits to designer suits and is very easy to get totally lost in.

Other well-known department stores include the bustling **Bloomingdales**, **Saks Fifth Avenue**, the stylish **Bergdorf Goodman** and the very elegant boutique-looking **Henri Bendel**. The label-conscious head to **Barneys** or the trendy boutiques in SoHo, while bargain hunters in search of labels-for-less regularly trawl **Century 21**. International designers are all represented in New York and it is sheer heaven just walking around some of these wonderfully opulent, bordering on decadent shops. Some of the greats include **Calvin Klein**, **Emporio Armani**, **Givenchy**, **Paul Smith**, **Romeo Gigli & Spazio**, **Yohji Yamamoto**, **Issey Miyake** and **Yves Saint Laurent**. On the other hand most would not want to miss the down-home trendy shopping at **Canal Jeans**, **The Gap** (literally on every other street corner), **New York Leather Company**, **The Original Levi Store**, **Patricia Field**, **Urban Outfitters** and **Banana Republic**. For great second-hand items try the sweet **Alice Underground** and **Harriet Love**.

New York has got to be a book lover's paradise. The **Barnes & Noble** chain has huge, wonderful shops all over the city where you can relax on cushy sofas and chairs and read anything you fancy to your heart's content. Many of these shops also have café bars and gloriously well-stocked music departments. Other well-travelled book shops include **Doubleday's**, **Gotham Book Mart**, the **Rizzoli** chain, and the terrific second-hand **Strand Book Store**.

Walkmans, computers and the like can be purchased for fair prices at **J & R Computer World**, while cameras, electronics and other goodies can be found at the famous **47th St Photo**.

Other famous New York shopping stops include **Hammacher Schlemmer** for unique gifts for the person who has everything but wants something else and the world renowned **FAO Schwarz** for just about every conceivable children's toy and game in the world.

Bed, Bath and Beyond is a good place to stock up on things linen, while **Pottery Barn**, **Crate And Barrel** and **Williams-Sonoma** are the shops for household and kitchen goods.

Music stores are mega in New York with fabulous choices that make one's head spin. Two of the biggest and best are **HMV** and **Tower Records**.

MUSEUMS

Whitney Museum of American Art

Wealthy sculptor and arts patron Gertrude Vanderbilt Whitney founded the Whitney Museum of American Art in her studio in a converted stable in MacDougal Alley in Greenwich Village after the **Metropolitan Museum of Art** rejected her collection. Today, visitors to Madison Avenue can see a constantly changing exhibition of 20th-century works by Andy Warhol, Edward Hopper, Andrew Wyeth and Jasper Johns. Almost all of America's leading artists in the last 50 years have been represented here in some way. Such is the significance of the collection housed here, that the museum is now regarded as a showcase for new trends in American art and remains strongly non-conformist.

The Museum of Modern Art

The Museum of Modern Art (MoMA) housing possibly the world's best collection of late-19th and 20th-century art in a fabulous glass and steel building on West 53rd Street, takes a liberal view of what constitutes art. This was the first museum to collect photography, film, industrial design and architectural work and display them alongside the more conventional types of artwork, thus providing a more comprehensive guide to the development of modern art and setting it in context with developments in other media of the same period. Works by Cézanne, Rodin, Picasso, Van Gogh and Matisse sit alongside such surrealist objects as a fur lined teacup, saucer and spoon challenging perceptions of the norm.

Museum of the City of New York

Housed in a custom-built mansion on the edge of Spanish Harlem, the Museum of the City of New York is dedicated solely to the life of the city and the people who live there, from the poor to the ridiculously wealthy. John D Rockefeller's bedroom, one of the period rooms housed in the museum, shows how the other half lived at the end of the 19th century.

The museum was established in 1923 as an attempt to educate New Yorkers about their heritage. Period rooms, the city's history, costumes, furniture silver, the history of musical theatre, toys and dolls houses dating from 1769 make this museum a place as much for children as adults.

The Cloisters

The Cloisters is probably the best example of building recycling around. Remains of medieval European churches and cloisters, shipped over to New York by John D Rockefeller and George Barnard, have been incorporated into an atmospheric building in **Fort Tryon Park** that houses the **Metropolitan Museum of Art**'s medieval collection. It is no surprise that this building is world famous for its medieval art since it contains a set of the Unicorn Tapestries, woven in Brussels around 1500, along with the *Belles Heures*, a prayer book containing 94 miniatures embellished in gold. Exhibits are arranged chronologically, beginning in 1000AD and ending around 1520AD and moving through frescoes, sculptures, stained glass and magnificent paintings.

American Museum of Natural History

Opened by President Ulysees Grant, the main entrance to this museum is a shrine to the work of this unrelenting campaigner, explorer and conservationist. Brontosauri, pterodactyls and other prehistoric creatures have been given a new lease of life in the recently opened dinosaur galleries at the American Museum of Natural History. Not all is skin and bones at this family favourite – also on display are thousands of other goodies, from the Star of India, the world's largest sapphire, to Native American artifacts and a full-scale reproduction of a blue whale .

The Metropolitan Museum of Art (Met)

The Metropolitan Museum of Art, usually known as the Met, contains more than three and a half million works of art from around the world. Established in 1870 to rival the world's art institutions, this is the place to indulge your interests and marvel at artworks from all over the world. The exhibits date from the prehistoric to the modern day. The collection includes suits of armour, ancient statues, African art, one of Rembrandt's self-portraits, Van Gogh's late works to photographs, clothes, modern American art and even a re-creation of a Frank Lloyd Wright room. Not to be missed is the popular Egyptian wing housing a treasure trove of works including the Temple of Dendur and models recovered on an archaelogical expedition sponsored by the Met. It is impossible to cover more than a fraction of the museum's collection at each visit, and also impossible not to get lost in this maze of a building.

Notes

Solomon R Guggenheim Museum

Apart from its brilliant collection of Kandinskys, Klees, Picassos and Calders, the Solomon R Guggenheim Museum is a work of art in its own right. Designed by American  architect Frank Lloyd Wright in 1943, but not completed until 1959, the museum had a controversial beginning, delayed initially because of disagreements with the planning authorities, the museum caused uproar among the public when it opened its doors. The abstract art on display and the interior of the building proved both controversial and sensational at the same time.

The building's most outstanding feature is its huge spiral gallery, which sometimes has more impact than the art on display. This is the place to see modern and contemporary art by leading artists from the 19th and 20th centuries. Start at the top in the huge glass dome and work your way down the spiral ramp through exhibits ranging from the museum's collection of impressionist and post-impressionist work, German expressionist paintings, historic *avant garde* artworks, minimalist art from the 60s and 70s and a sculpture terrace.

The Brooklyn Museum

Standing next door to the beautiful **Brooklyn Botanic Gardens** is the Brooklyn Museum, which has recently been revamped and contains important Egyptian artifacts and some charming period rooms. It is hard to believe that this museum is not yet complete since it houses an exhaustive 1.5 million exhibits. Not to be missed are the collection of native American art, the 28 period rooms and a breathtaking art collection. The exhibits are spread over five floors, with galleries covering everything from classical, decorative and Egyptian art, sculpture, paintings, murals, prints, photographs, drawings, Asian, African, Oceanic and New World art. The museum developed from the Brooklyn Apprentice's Library Association, the acting librarian of which in 1835 was a lad called Walt Whitman.

FINAL THOUGHTS

Museums & History

American Museum of Natural History, Central Park West & 79th St

American Museum of the Moving Image, 35th Ave at 36th St, Astoria, Queens

Brooklyn Museum, 200 Eastern Parkway

Chinatown History Museum, 70 Mulberry St

The Cloisters, Fort Tryon Park

Cooper-Hewitt National Design Mus, 2 E 91st St, at 5th Ave

Ellis Island (immigration museum) New York Harbour

Ellis Island, ferry from Battery Park

Federal Hall Museum, 4881 Broadway & 204th St

Federal Hall, 28 Wall St

Forbes Magazine Galleries, 62 5th Ave at 12th St

Fraunces Tavern, 54 Pearl St

Frick Collection, 1 E 70th St

Intrepid Sea-Air-Space Museum, 86 12th Ave & W 46th St

Library and Museum of Performing Arts, Lincoln Center, 11 Amsterdam Av & W 65th St

Lower East Side Tenement Museum, 97 Orchard St

Metropolitan Museum of Art, 5th Ave & E 82nd St

Morris-Jumel Mansion, 1765 Jumel Terrace, between W 160th & W 162nd St

Museum of American Folk Art, 2 Lincoln Square & 65th St & Columbus Ave

Museum of Modern Art, 11 W 53rd St

Museum of the City of New York, 5th Ave & 103rd St

Pierpont Morgan Library, 29 E 36th St

Schlomburg Center for Research in Black Culture, 515 Malcolm X Boulevard

Solomon R Guggenheim Museum, 1071 5th Ave

South Street Seaport Museum, 12 Fulton St, & Front St

Theodore Roosevelt Birthplace Museum, 28 E 20th St
United Nations, 1st Ave & 46th St
Whitney Museum of American Art, Madison Ave & 75th St

Architecture & Skyline
Brooklyn Bridge
Chrysler Building, Lexington Ave, 42nd St
The Chanin, Lexington Ave, 42nd St
Cooper Union Building, 41 Cooper Square
Empire State Building, 350 5th Ave & 34th St
Flatiron Building, 175 5th Ave
General Electric Building, 570 Lexington Ave
Grand Central Terminal, 42nd St & Park Ave
Lever House, Park Ave & 54th St
National Arts Club, 15 Gramercy Park
New York Public Library, 5th Ave & 42nd St
Rockefeller Center, between 5th & 6th Ave & 47th & 51st St
Seagram Building, Park Ave & 52nd St
Trump Tower, 725 5th Avenue
Twin Towers, Central Park West
Woolworth Building, 233 Broadway
World Trade Center, between Church & Liberty St

Shopping
47th Street Photo, 67 W 47th St
Alice Underground, 481 Broadway & Broome St
Banana Republic, various locations
Barnes & Noble, 105 5th Ave & 18th St
Barneys, 106 7th Ave, between W 17th St & W 18th St
Bed, Bath and Beyond, 620 6th Ave & 18th St
Bergdorf Goodman, 754 5th Ave & 58th St
Bloomingdales, 1000 3rd Ave & E 59th St

Canal Jeans, 504 Broadway
Century 21 Department Store, 22 Cortlandt St
Calvin Klein, 654 Madison Ave & 60th St
Crate & Barrel, 650 Madison Ave & 59th St
Doubleday's, 724 5th Ave & 57th St
Emporio Armani, 110 5th Ave & 16th St
FAO Schwarz, 767 5th Ave & 58th St
Givenchy, 954 Madison Ave & 75th St
Gotham Book Mart, 41 W 47th St near 6th Ave
Hammacher Schlemmer, 147 East 57th St
Harriet Love, 126 Prince St
Henri Bendel, 714 5th Avenue & 56th St
HMV, various locations
Issey Miyake, 992 Madison Ave between 77th & 78th St
J & R Computer World & Music World, 134 Park Row
Lord & Taylor, 424 5th Ave between 38th & 39th St
Macy's, Herald Square, 151 W 34th St
Mulberry Street, Little Italy
New York Leather Company, 33 Christopher St
Patricia Field, 10 E 8th St, near 5th Avenue
Paul Smith, 108 5th Ave between 15th & 16th St
Pottery Barn, various locations
Rizzoli, various locations
Rockefeller Center
Romeo Gigli & Spazio, 21 E 69th St
Saks Fifth Avenue, 611 5th Ave between 49th & 50th St
South Street Seaport
Strand Book Store at 828 Broadway, E 12th St
The Original Levi Store, 750 Lexington Ave & 59th St
Tower Records, various locations
Union Square Greenmarket
Urban Outfitters, various locations

Williams-Sonoma, various locations
Willoughby's, 136 W 32nd St & 6th & 7th Avenue
Yohji Yamamoto, 103 Grand St, near Broadway
Yves Saint Laurent, 855–9 Madison Ave between E 70th
and 71st St

Eating & Drinking

An American Place, 2 Park Ave at E 32nd St
Café des Artistes, 1 W 67th St at Central Park West
Carnegie Delicatessen, 854 7th Ave near 55th St
Chanterelle, 2 Harrison St
Dean & DeLuca, 560 Broadway at Prince St
E Js Luncheonette, 447 Amsterdam Ave & 81st St
Four Seasons, 99 E 52nd St
Golden Unicorn, 18 East Broadway
Gotham Bar & Grill, 12 E 12th St near 5th Avenue
Grand Central Oyster Bar, Grand Central Station
H&H Bagel, 1551 2nd Avenue between 80th and 81st St
Hard Rock Café, 221 W 57th St
Katz's Deli, 205 E Houston St
Kiev Luncheonette, 117 2nd Ave
Le Café Figaro, 184 Bleecker St
Le Cirque, Mayfair Baglioni Hotel, 58 E 65th St near
Madison Ave
Les Halles, 411 Park Ave
McSorley's Old Alehouse, 15 E 7th St between 2nd & 3rd Ave
Mesa Grill, 102 5th Ave
Michael's Pub, 211 E 55th St
Nobu, 105 Hudson St & Franklin St
Oak Room and Bar, The Plaza, 768 5th Avenue
P J Clarke's, 915 3rd Avenue
River Café, 1 Water St, Brooklyn

Royalton Hotel, 44 W 44th St between 5th & 6th Ave
Second Avenue Deli, 156 2nd Ave at 10th St
Sign of the Dove, 1110 3rd Ave at 65th St
St Regis Hotel
Stage Deli, 834 7th Ave
Tenth Street Lounge, 212 E 10th St between 1st & 2nd Ave
The Algonquin Hotel, 59 W 44th St
The Ear Inn, 326 Spring St
The Rainbow Room, Rockefeller Center, Rockefeller Place
Tribeca Grill, 375 Greenwich St at Franklin St
Union Square Café, 21 E 16th St between Union Square
and 5th Ave
Zabar's Café, 2245 Broadway & 80th St

Entertainment
Alice Tully Hall, Lincoln Center
Angelika Film Center, 18 W Houston St
Avery Fisher Hall, Lincoln Center
Bargemusic, Fulton Ferry Landing, Brooklyn
Brooklyn Academy of Music, 30 Lafayette St, Brooklyn
Carnegie Hall, 156 W 57th St
CBGB, 315 Bowery
Chamber Music Society, Lincoln Center
City Center Theater, 131 W 55th St between 6th & 7th Ave
Cotton Club, 666 W 125th St
Dance Theater Workshop, 219 W 19th St
Dance Theatre of Harlem, 466 W 152nd St
Juilliard School of Music, Lincoln Center
Knitting Factory, 74 Leonard St between Broadway
& Church St
Merce Cunningham Studio, 55 Bethune St between
Washington and West St

Metropolitan Opera House, Lincoln Center
New York State Theater, Lincoln Center
PS122, 150 1st Ave & 9th St
Public Theater, 425 Lafayette St
Radio City Music Hall, 1260 6th Ave at 50th St
Shea Stadium, Flushing Meadows
Vivian Beaumont Theater, Lincoln Center
Wollman Rink, Central Park
Yankee Stadium, River Ave & 161st St
92nd Street Y, 1395 Lexington Ave at 92nd St

Sights, Parks and Churches
Cathedral of St John the Divine, Amsterdam Ave at 112th St
Central Park
Gramercy Park, 20th St
IBM Building courtyard, 590 Madison Ave
Little Church around the Corner, 1 E 29th St
New York Botanical Garden, 200th St & Southern Boulev'd
New York Public Library, 5th Ave & 42nd St
Pier 17, South Street Seaport
St Patrick's Cathedral, 5th Ave & 50th St
Statue of Liberty, ferry from Battery Park
Times Square, Broadway & W 42nd St
Washington Square Arch

Museum Quilts would like to thank the following people whose assistance contributed to
the preparation of this book.

Notions Antiquaria, 24 Cecil Court, Charing Cross Road, London WC2.

Tracy Brett, 174 Oldfield Grove, London SE16.

Michael Finney, Antique Books and Prints, 11 Camden Passage, Islington, London N1.

Designed by Gordon Parker & John Casey

Published by Museum Quilts (UK) Inc.
254-258 Goswell Road, London EC1V 7EB

ISBN: 1-897954-44-1

Printed and bound in Spain

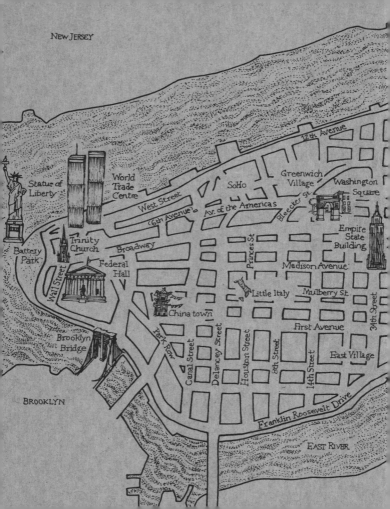